Tacos and Gumbo Productions

FIST & FIRE
Poems to inspire action and ignite passion

LESLE' HONORE'

FIST & FIRE

Leslé Honoré

Dedication

I am possible because of my parents, Louis and Rosalba Honoré. My father's love of story, on paper, in song, in film, my mother's strength and unbreakable joy. They have both have imprinted on me and helped me carve a path when I was the most lost and hopeless. They planted seeds of survival in my soul. I am able to write because of them.

I am possible because of my children. With their first breaths I understood my purpose in life. With each of their births I was born again. My Sage helps me find peace. My Bubba helps me find wisdom. My Scarlett reminds me to live with reckless abandon. I can dream because of them.

I am possible because of my friends. Rhonda and Angie have shown me what loyalty is, what a village is, they are what hope and faith looks like. Michelle H, Sarah H and Sara M have shown me what a soft place to fall feels like. David has taught me how freedom and self-love can redefine you. Rai and Sylvia have taught me, that family can be born on another continent and find you still. Isa has helped my soul dance into the universe and Brother Mike's laughter will always guide me. I can love because of all of you.

I am possible because of my aunts, uncles and army of cousins in Mexico's warm sun and Louisiana's music-filled air. Don, Deidra, Bryan, Ken, Kenny, Andy, Albert, Irene and Phil, you epitomize our generations, our differences, the blood and truth that binds us all. I am connected because of you.

I am possible because of my Xavier Family. My #PettyXU crew, Dr. Michelle Levy, Anika G, you all remind me to keep dreaming my dreams. I celebrate your successes like they are my own, and they push me to work harder. You see, in me, what is possible. I hope to make you proud.

I am, because of love and pain. Fred, you taught me to be grateful for both. Your love freed me. You convinced me that I had wings. I believed you. I am flying, touching the sky. Forever your Birdy.

I am possible because of my niece, Destiny; who reminds me that how we love defines us, how we give reflects our hearts, how we forgive influences our integrity, and how we persevere makes us a woman to admire. I am in awe of the woman she has become. I am a better person because of her. Every poem, verse, word and letter in this book is possible because of Destiny. If I birthed it, she is the midwife.

I am possible because of my sister Lolita. My twin soul. Our voices, script, humor, hope, love, fears, faith and dreams are all intertwined. The farther we have gotten away from each other, the more God showed us that we can not split the atom, that is us without devastating fall out. She is not my cheerleader but a stadium full of love and encouragement. She is a compass for my dreams and the voice that made me believe that greatness is possible, that this book was possible, that I am possible. My dream is possible because of her belief in me when I could not muster it; Her vision when I was blind to it; And her faith that helped me grow my own. I can stand while gale force winds surround me because she is by my side. This book is dedicated to all of you. Because of all of you. I humbly thank you.

Fist

Fire

Lagniappe

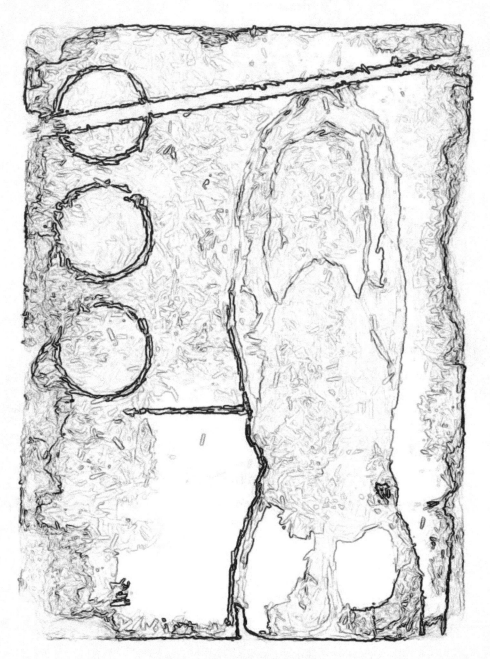

FIST

and the light dims

little girls are light
the moment we know
our wombs house them
they become our glow
we wrap them in pink blankets
brown skin
radiating love
and soon
when the words come
so do the questions
can i have this doll?
the one with the yellow hair
and blue eyes?
she's beautiful
can i be beautiful?
can my pony tail hang down my back?
why can't i have hair like her?
and the light dims
and soon
when the understanding comes
the self-hate flutters in
like a colonial moth
on wings of oppression
at school there are no books with me
with my skin

my nose
my hair
i'm not pretty
and the light dims
and soon
womanhood
dances around their youth
hand outstretched
inviting them to sway
dancing to melodies
that sound like independence
the anger comes
he accused me of cheating
me
i've never had an average under a 98
he accused me
in front of the class
the entire class
he says he only dates
white girls
light girls
they asked if my hair is real
if they could touch it
they did
i didn't say they could
they called me ghetto
they called me nigger

why did that man just call my mother
girl
and the light dims
and we mothers weep
into our pillows
in the shower
in the car
tears we know they will shed too
because the world hasn't changed
behind our desks
solitary and alone
the only woman
the only brown
the only other
and we are asked to
educate
explain
be the voice of our people
why do "you people"
say?
do?
act?
can you explain rap?
what's a chitterling?
work place mammies
wet nurses
breasts filled

with black trauma
suckling ignorance
promotions passing us by
like tides that never reach our shores
and our supposed 70 cents on the dollar
is undoubtedly less
in our black checks
but we can't prove it
and our light dims
we balance our love
on titanium backs
with feet cemented in
"this won't be my daughter's life"
we turn ourselves
inside out
no sacrifice too great
to help them spread wings
not weighed down by their blackness
but fueled by it
but their feet sometimes are tethered to
an earth filled with welfare queen lies
because brown girls can't fly
too high
can't soar above
yellow hair
if they do
they might swing from an imaginary

noose
too short for their 6 foot body
and die for not signaling a lane change
when you say
all lives matter
i ask
will your daughter be sexualized
before she bleeds
will her brilliance always be doubted
will she always be marginalized
race and sex intersecting like knife in flesh
will your 5 year old
whisper in your ear
while wrapped in your loving arms
"raquel says i'm too dark to be pretty"
will your daughter hate her own skin
mine have
black girls matter too

backpacks

when black boys are born
we mothers kiss their faces
twirl our fingers in their curls
put them in carriers on our chest
show them to the world
our tiny black princes
and when they start school
as early as 3
we mothers
place huge backpacks on their backs
and we slowly fill them with *bricks*
etched with tools
tattooed with truths
hoping to save them
don't talk back
don't get angry
say yes ma'am
say no sir
don't fight
even if they hit you first
especially if they are white
do your best
better than best
be still
work hardest

brick

they get a little older

and we add more

keep your hands out of your pockets

don't look them in the eye

don't challenge

don't put your manhood before your life

just get home safe

don't walk alone

don't walk with too many boys

don't walk towards police

don't walk away from police

don't buy candy or iced tea

don't put your hood up

i'll drive you

i'll pick you up

you can't be free

don't go wandering

come home to me

brick

they get a little older

and we add more

understand you are a threat

standing still

breathing

your degrees are not a shield

your job is not a shield

your salary makes you a target
your car makes you a target
your nice house in a nice neighborhood
makes you a target
don't put your ego before your safety
don't talk back
don't look them in the eye
get home to your wife
your son
brick
they weigh them down
this knowing
of having to carry the load
of their blackness
the world hasn't changed
the straps just dig deeper into their skin
their backs ache
but their souls don't break
our beautiful black men
when you say to me
all lives matter
i simply ask
will your son die with the world on his back
mine will

chitown fruit

chicago streets bear a strange fruit
blood on the leaves
and blood at the root
black bodies rotting
in the lake shore breeze
strange fruit trampled
in the chitown streets
past madison headed south
the bulging eyes and the twisted mouth
sight of blue lights flashing bright
then 16 shots ring into the night
here is a fruit for the pigs to pluck
for the boots to kick
lifeless bodies are cuffed
for mayor to ignore
city hall will cover up
here is a strange and bitter crop

for chicago

your tiny hands
can't reach the
broad shoulders
that bear the burdens
of this city
your tiny mind
can't comprehend
the magnitude
of the heartache
in this city
policing is nothing but
a blue-uniformed
band-aid
the hemorrhaging blood
flowing in the streets
a parallel river of pain
that can't be dyed green
is a symptom
not the problem
this city is sick
it has a cancer
a tumor triggered by
segregation
food deserts
school closures
poverty

hopelessness
pain of being invisible
to city hall's sympathy
if you are brown and black
if you live too far south of madison
if you are brown and black
if you live too far west of state
if you are brown and black
if you are brown and black
your life is filled with
inequity and lack
your orange dust-colored soul
doesn't love this city
you don't know the joy
of a 60 degree day
in the middle of january
the rapture of a summer sunday
the rhythm of a drum beat
on the red line
symphonies under the stars
street vendors
socks to tamales
fruit chews and bean pies
a maxwell street polish
and a man who wants to save your soul
can all be found on the streets of the 'go
all of this and more

is what your toupee-topped mind
doesn't know
stay the hell out my city
our many imperfections
aren't in need of militarization
the feds
aren't the
meds
we need
we already have enough
murder in the name of protection
we don't need any more shots
16 are more than enough
we have our own fleet
on the streets
fighting for
our city
our streets
our lives
your hands are too small
your arms are too short
to box with these chicago gods
keep your tiny hands away from my city
keep chicago's name out of your mouth
#16shots

hope

the day is dreary, blustery and gray, but warm for
january in chicago.

i'm sipping some chai, in a starbucks in hyde park. a
few doors down from valois, my favorite breakfast spot,
and yours as well.

the windows are covered. the news vans outside. the
barriers are up.

you'll be here soon. lester holt will interview you.

the people outside, bundled and waiting, will hope for a
glimpse of you. a wave. a smile. and if the gods are
good, a selfie.

i remember being outside valois in 2008. it was
november and 70 degrees. strangers hugged. horns
honked. we were singing in the streets... no really we
were! (think "brand new day" from the wiz)

i stood there with my little family. my husband and
children, they were 8, 5 and 3 months. all of us without
any clue of what the next 8 years would bring.

my husband leaving me to raise them alone

unemployment

foreclosure

loss of friends

gaining of new ones

love

death

but always there was hope.

you were hope

your wife was hope

your daughters were hope

a real black family in beautiful shades of brown walking
hand in hand to a victory none of us thought was
possible. except for that tiny bit of hope in the tiniest
corner of our souls.

as my marriage ended, as our family changed, you were
hope. not cosby show scripted, but a real father who
looked at his daughters as if they wore his dreams like
crowns in their hair. a real husband who looked at his
wife like she was his oxygen.

i have never seen such adoration.

you were an image of a father to the fatherless,
successes to the fighters still in the trenches. you were
the embodiment that representation matters. my
children have only ever really known a black president.
without scandal. with one family. with the hope of a
nation on his shoulders.

there will be tons of books that will be written that
deconstruct your administration, your many failures
and the multitude of successes that white supremacy
will ignore and try to suppress.

but in this moment as i sit filled with hope to see your
motorcade again, or catch a glimpse of your smile, i
separate the man and the politician.

i am filled with gratitude for a man who is the epitome
of grace, integrity, class, joy, perseverance, dignity and
above all hope.

#alwaysmypresident

eulogy for hope

we mourn today because hope is leaving

we are not mourning the loss of hillary

because let's be honest,

we really wanted bernie

but we said ok

let's elect this woman

we will make this work

because we are resourceful.

resilient

we survived the middle passage

slavery

jim crow

civil rights

assassination of almost all of our leaders

we overcome, that's what we do

(but don't start singing that weak ass song)

we mourn today because we gave this country a little

piece of hope

when obama became president

even though he endured disrespect

ugliness

nasty venom

aimed not just at him but at his

daughters

and his wife

we still began to hope

that maybe this nation was more

than what we knew it to be

hate-filled

ignorant

illiterate

that despises anyone

who is not

male

straight

white

and christian

we mourn the end of 8 years

where we couldn't be prouder of our leader

today

we mourn.

dear 53 % white women who voted for trump,
how do we get rid of our vaginas so we can get
insurance ?
asking for my daughters

ps
how do you sleep at night ?
do your mothers and grandmothers haunt you ?
or do your ancestors know that you are trash so they
don't visit ?

psa... for mofos irritated about poems i pen about their precious president and his crew

for 8 years i heard and saw ignorant, racist people say

every heinous thing they could about the obamas, not

because they were liars

or sexist

or narcissist

or evil

or rapist

but because barack and michelle are black

educated and black

successful and black

brilliant and black

so "trust and believe"

i will point out every single one

of trump's flaws

and those of his wife

his adult children

his cabinet

his friends

his supporters

every damn day for the next 4 years

if i have to

not because they are white

or because they are republicans

but because they are,
to quote auntie maxine waters
"scumbags"
the entire lot of them
and also because
i am pretty and petty
because i am an artist
because art is activism
because my black revolutionary jesus
called me to
because nina simone
said i must reflect the times
because frida painted the ugly
and made you look at it and
find beauty in it
... but mainly because i will never forget
what you said about my president
what you said about his family
what you have said about us
my soul has a touch of arya stark
the north remembers
your names have been on my lips
petty prayers of vengeance
my pen has just begun
#cantstopwontstop

i will not stay calm.
i have a black boy.

trash of a mama

our mamas taught us how to sit

to wear slips

pantyhose

cross our legs at the ankle

our mamas taught us how to act

how to respect ourselves

our homes

our bodies

our mamas taught us

that how we act in public

was a reflection of our whole family

we would never kneel

on someone's furniture

put our shoes on someone's couch

we would never spread our legs

in the oval office

we would never be filth

in the white house

our mamas taught us

money can't buy class

just because you are poor

you don't have to be trash

how to remove our makeup

with ponds every night

to help keep our face soft

keep our skin smooth and tight

our mamas taught us

the difference between

the truth and a lie

how to hold our heads high

to never support a man

who thinks less of you

kellyanne what did your trash of a mama

teach you?

GOP meal plan

have you ever been hungry?

have you ever been poor?

have you ever thought to yourself

i know they'll have breakfast and lunch at school?

have you ever taught a hungry kid

with headaches and sharp stomach pains?

have you ever been hungry?

it's hard to think when you are hungry

when you are hungry it's hard to learn

you don't care if the pizza tastes like cardboard

or the chicken has no flavor

you just know when you get home

there is nothing on your table

have you ever held on to the

apples and oranges

the milk and crackers

that other kids don't eat

so you can tuck them in

some baby's backpack

for their younger siblings

or because it's friday

and you know weekends are hard

and long with no food

have you ever been hungry?

not i-skipped-breakfast

i'm on a diet

i left my wallet

but hungry

my mama ain't working

she sold the stamps to pay rent

my mama gone

my daddy gone

my granny sick

there is nothing but ice in the ice box

i like going to school because there i can eat

have you ever looked in a child's eyes

and seen that type of hungry look back at you

have you ever hugged a child

and felt their stomach growl through their back?

have you ever been hungry?

mick mulvaney

i hope you die hungry

we already made america great

on our backs

with our blood

on our souls

with our hands

on our shoulders

with our strength

with our tears

with our ancestors

and our legacies

on our hopes

with our will

on our prayers

with our courage

on our screams

with your lash

on our scars

on our lives

with our might

with our genius

with our light

with our magic

in spite of your hate

the children of slaves

have already made america great

word wet nurse

i have been struggling with my words

and i rarely struggle with my words

this election

this nation

this world

has me feeling too much

i remember when my babies were nursing

at the end of the day i would feel touched out

the moments were blissful

but in between the love

were spaces of time

where all i wanted was my body back

just for myself

too many touches

too many needy mouths

lives that were more important than my own

i feel like that now that i have been a "word wet nurse"

trying to nourish the ignorant

neglecting my own infants

and when i look at their faces

expectant for explanation

i have nothing but bitter truths

this world isn't for us

they don't want us

they just want our milk

#wetnursetoamericasince1619

do you cry yourself to sleep at night worrying that every year he ages, every day he gets closer to manhood?

pleading the blood

many a mother of black boys
pleaded the blood of jesus over them
many a mother of black boys
instilled the faith of god in them
many a mother of black boys
still
buried their black boys
covered
in the blood of jesus
which was covered
in black boy's blood
which mothers then
covered
with dirt and tombstone
mary wept at her black boy's tomb too
i will not stay calm. i have a black boy. and if you do not
have a black boy, you will not check my rage or my fear.
not with your condescension and not with your god.

bull's eye

our sons are men

the moment they fall from our

wombs

the moment their skin becomes

tan

or brown

or black

our sons are men

the moment they open their eyes

the moment they live

the moment they breathe

and your whiteness sees them as threat

your boys stay boys well into their 30s

they can blow up oklahoma

slaughter a church

rape at will

eat faces like pancakes at ihop

destroy gas stations in rio

and run home to their mommies

you will post their best graduation pictures

explain that they are mentally ill

say that they have made mistakes

that boys will be boys

and they deserved time for redemption

my sons are given 2 seconds with a toy gun

2 minutes with their hands in the air

a hoodie and a handful of candy

is a death sentence

because my sons

are men at

12

17

18

and targets at birth

no justice no peace

they keep calling for peace
france didn't call for peace when their people were
slaughtered
they bombed hospitals. babies dead.
9/11 didn't call for peace.
we went to war. invaded. murdered. created imaginary
weapons of mass destruction.
but our people are dead in the streets
their murders on repeat on tv
to desensitize us
make us forget that
17 is a boy
12 is a child
9 is a baby
imagine the peace in the city if rahm's son was killed
fuck your peace
call for it in your own depraved souls
call for it in your uniformed murderers
call for it in your government willing to look the other
way on a child's slaughter to win an election
fuck your peace
we are calling for justice

crime and punishment

in this country
on the planet
it's a crime to be black
it's a crime to be black
it's a crime to be black
punishable by death

hashtags

we are not people

we are hashtags

targets

shapes to outline with chalk

we are not

fathers and mothers

we are bad dudes

crazy

suicidal

non-compliant

we are not children

we are juvenile delinquents

gang bangers

hooded threats

monsters

we have never been

more than 3/5 human

on this soil

no matter how we beat back headlines

with our brilliance

our magic

we are still lynched in the streets

when we cry out in pain

this nation demands

silence

we publicize

go live

record

report

our pain

our blood flowing like rivers

and it makes no difference

killers will be

indicted

never convicted

blue freedom

over

black lives

repetitively

black death the new groundhog day

black people magic

freddie gray
was so magical
that he severed his own spine
crushed his own voice box
killed himself. alone. handcuffed
sandra was so magical
that she hung herself
with invisible trash bags
from an unseen rafter
taller than her
6 foot frame
tamir was a wizard
that turned his toy gun
into an ak in less than 2 seconds
mike brown was a sorcerer
who could transform into a monster
who could stand still
hands in the air
and threaten a man with a gun
and eric garner was so filled with ancestral power
he didn't need air to breathe
don't you see

unless we call the ministry of magic

there will never be a conviction in these courts

another magician once told us

"the master's tools will never dismantle master's house"

- audre lorde

never to be men

today you would have been 21
full of emerging manhood
and the bravado of "legality"
your long legs striding
head held high
dazzling smile
21 means freedom
what every teen can't wait to achieve
you would have crossed
the imaginary line into adulthood
today
instead of your first drink
or candles blown with wishes
we take a drink to quiet sorrow
light candles in memoriam
with an all too familiar ache
we say your name
and the names of the brown boys
who have gone before you
the multitudes of brown boys slain
after we laid you to rest

our boys

never to be men

innocent

their only guilt

melanin

happy birthday trayvon

innocence uprooted

my bubba built guns out of barbie legs

legos

toast

and when all else failed...his fingers

he was han solo.

no force needed. just a blaster

tamir could have been my bubba

shooting at imaginary bad guys

at a park

at play

hands in his pockets to stay warm

2 seconds from squad car to murder

the light of 1000 make-believe dreams shone in his eyes

because that's what 12 year old boys look like...

imagination sprinkled with dirt

feet firmly planted in childhood

like roots in earth of innocence

not even their tallest branches reach for manhood yet

he was 12

he was no threat

his hands in his pockets

someone's baby like my baby boy

can you feel us?
we hope for you

tyshawn lee

i don't care if his mama bought a car with donated
money.
or if his daddy was in every gang on the south side
he was nine.
he was executed.
someone looked him in his face and shot him
multiple times
in his uniform
on his way to his granny's house
he probably smelled like outside.
free and happy on a warm autumn day
maybe he had a great day at school
did well on a test
got student of the week
his crush smiled at him
he was nine
full of little boy dreams
maybe he liked legos
or xmen
or mine craft
pizza and ice cream
maybe he wanted a hover-board for christmas or his

birthday

miss me with crucifying the parents

y'all sheep keep following everything the world keeps

tossing at you to make you forget

make you no longer see his innocence.

his humanity

if his skin wasn't brown the entire world would be

weeping

he was nine

be outraged about that

#tyshawnlee

no convictions

good morning.
it's groundhog day.
no officers will be indicted in connection with the death
of sandra bland
if you are surprised... wake the fuck up !
the death of our men mean nothing
our women are strange fruit in jail cells
our daughters slammed to the ground while sitting in
their desks
our sons slaughtered while our mayor
suppresses the evidence so he can win an election, and
the day the video is released he lights a christmas tree.
it's repetitious. cyclical.
with the desired effect to numb you
did it work ?
are you still outraged ?
do you still mourn them ?
do you still say their names ?
#sandrabland #16shots #say theirnames

comprehension

we believe you

you hate us

you don't have to continue to prove it

you don't have to continue to slaughter us

shoot us

strangle us

billy club us

we know there will be no justice

there will be no conviction

there will be no succor for alton's 5 children

we know you fear us

we know you fear us

we know you fear us

and you should

our rage is a righteous one

like volcanic eruptions

a revolutionary pompeii is coming

this earth for too long

has been saturated with the blood of us

air thick with the screams of us

and when we explode

not even the name

of your white god will save you

you will look at his face

and you will only see us

#altonsterling

crucifixions

philando would have been 33 today
i know another black man
lynched by roman police
when he was 33
for being a revolutionary
and the politicians washed their hands of
that death too

america breeds
a special kind of hate

lavish

lavish reynolds

eye in hurricane center calm

mama with baby in the back seat

saving your own life

you don't move

you don't stop

showing the world

horror

hands still up

we cry for you

lavish reynolds

loving your black man

your life line

your best friend

saying his name

we scream for you

lavish reynolds

dignity surrounded by none

truth surrounded by none

strength surrounded by none

we reach for you

with black and brown and beige hands

with black and brown and beige hearts

echoing your daughter's words

"it's ok sister, we are here"

can you feel us?

we hope for you

#philandocastile

serve and protect?

i don't care how many tattoos he had
if his grill was all gold
how far his pants sagged
how many profile pics of guns are on his page
he did not deserve death
he did not deserve murder
he did not deserve to be handcuffed while
lifeless
he did not deserve your boot
stomping him
lifeless
he did not deserve to be
lifeless
he deserved due process
under the same laws you vow to uphold
you can't serve the law
and break the law
turn off your cameras
ask your partner if you were shot at
after
after
after

you murdered someone

you can't serve the law

while breaking the law

you can't step in our son's blood

and serve us ice cream cones

and expect us not to hate you

when warriors are supposed to only be men

i am expected

to suffer in silence

to weep for my sons and daughters

where you cannot hear my moans

i am expected to wear my skin

as a target

in shame

and to apologize for it

i am expected

to never break

endure the world

to fear but never act afraid

i am expected to send

my men

my sons

my daughters

to slaughter

and not take up arms

i am expected

to swirl the taste of my blood in my mouth

mixed with shots of your hatred

with a chaser of your oppression

and swallow

and enjoy it

and love you the more

for the forced pour

i am expected

not to protect my children

when you come into my home

guns drawn

false warrants thrown

i am expected to forsake my own

in the name of compliance

#korryngaines

the aria of betty jo shelby
sung in the key of privilege
to the tune of murder
with police brutality as the accompaniment
also known as the funeral dirge of
terence crutcher

i am a white woman

i can kill a black man

because his existence

made me fear for my life

i will be acquitted

stroll back to work

in less than a week

with my privilege

floating behind me

like a train on a wedding gown

mother of pearl white

stitched with the threads of my

complacency

i am a white woman

an assassin with

accusations as ammunition

always loaded

can't conceal

my weaponized whiteness

which i will value more

than any feminist agenda

i want to be equal with white men

not to brown and black women

i will break the glass ceilings

and watch them sweep up my mess

i am white woman

who will reign down a white hot heat

on any white wombs who dare

to step out of this lane

to be an ally

to fight for freedoms

to shout truths

to use their privilege

to amplify

to shield

to make safe spaces

to understand

i am a white woman

i know that this protects me

high on my pedestals

elevated innocence

aryan perfection

and no one will question my throne

because i can kill a black man for a whistle

i can kill a black man for a look

i can shoot a black man

stranded on the side of the road

with a stalled car

not because he pulled a weapon on me

lunged at me

threatened me

but because he looked like a

bad dude

i will serve no time

there will be no punishment

i will not mourn

a life less valuable than mine

because i am a white woman

#terencecrutcher

who is muted more than our kings?
only our slaughtered queens

for emmett

when the truth comes 62 years too late

some of you

not all of you

but some of you

tell lies

lies meant to kill

absolve your guilt

call undeserved attention

pull triggers

murder

with only your words

and some of you will wait

62 years after

your forked tongue

has not only

sent a 14 year old baby to his grave

but whispered the rally cry

like a bugle before war

that sent

men's fists

and boots

and bats

and barbed wire
to beat a baby boy
beyond recognition
and anchor him
to the bottom of a lake
some of you kill
with your lies
you don't have to raise a
dainty privilege pink hand
to point out an assailant that's fake
you simply open your mouth
your lie becomes
judge, jury and executioner
you make it rain
alternate truths
stepford-stride yourself
into a white house
drown your sons
in a car in a river
set off nationwide manhunts
for a black man
that didn't exist
your lies
imprison

steal scholarships

strip futures

seal a fate

with a pucker

you kill with your lies

you rob promotions

belittle children

appropriate

and acquire generational wealth

with your lies

you vote for a pussy-grabbing scum

and then march and sing

we shall overcome

some of you are allies

fighting by our side

but so many of you are darth susans

just filling the air with more lies

they are the lies that bury our boys

lies that elect hate

lies the stare us in our face

screaming fictional rape

some of you

not all of you

tell murderous lies

and walk away nonchalant

immune to our cries

and on your death bed

62 years later

you confess

and we are supposed to forgive

"negroes

sweet and docile,

meek, humble, and kind:

beware the day

they change their mind !"

~langston hughes

#carolynbryantdonham #susansmith

#jarretadams#jilliansheamoore

#leanneblack #scottsboroboys #kellyanneconway

#melaniatrump

look away dixieland

to kill a man

with black skin

isn't a sin

deep in the heart of dixie

bloody hands

are washed and cleaned

white innocence gleams

deep in the heart of dixie

white murderers go free

no jail

no parole

not even a plea

deep in the heart of dixie

but don't you march

or cry

or scream

fire hoses, dogs and bullets are a thrill

protestors will be shot at will

deep in the heart of dixie

"oh, i wish i was in the land of cotton,

old times there are not forgotten.

look away, look away, look away dixie land!"

#joemcknight

the string of blame

i know i am not the only one
who feels the weight of this city
heavy on my chest
tight in my throat
eyes swimming with tears
my soul screaming
i know i am not the only one
mourning for babies
that weren't born to me
but born of me
i know i am not the only one
who doesn't give a fuck
about what lavontay white jr.'s
family was involved in
i know that focusing on his uncle
or father
or mother
or neighborhood
only allows people to put the death
of a baby
in a place that doesn't bring them to their knees
they can place his blood

on the hands of thugs

on animals

on ghetto

and not turn over the blame that sits

in all of our laps

a pachyderm of problems

that we ignore

that murders babies

live on facebook

i know i am not the only one

that understands

that the string of blame goes like this

evil

middle passage

slavery

black codes

jim crow

segregation

systemic racism

red lining

ghettos

poverty

food deserts

crumbling schools

closing schools

poverty

hopelessness

rage

lost

mass incarceration

school to prison pipeline

anger

unemployment

hunger

cold

survival

chaos

a people with backs against the wall

fighting for forever

making choices no one wants to make

trauma

surrounded my constant trauma

and a nation who has called you

nothing

for longer than you can remember

so the nothing creeps into your spirit

and babies get shot

babies get shot babies get shot

and no one says their names

because the world already considered

them nothing too

i know i'm not the only one

who knows this

weeps for this

and i know i am not the only one

who knows that

police don't fight poverty

national guard doesn't restore hope

uniforms don't provide protection

they all just reinforce

that we are animals that need to be

controlled

and our babies

dead or alive

aren't mourned by them

because they are just

thugs in the making

i know i am not the only one

screaming in my soul

with a prayer for

lavontay white jr.

on my lips

four little girls and mine

as i brushed scarlett's hair this morning
trying to be gentle
braiding bits of my heart
into pig tails
smoothing the fuzzies
laying baby hairs
tying ribbons to match her dress
knowing that we only have a few more years
of bows and barrettes
8 will be 14 soon
i kiss her forehead and
i think
she will go into school feeling loved
looking loved
being love
and at 3:45
she will hop into our car
chatter about her day
annoy her siblings
i will take her home
my mind traveled
(being the vagabond that it is)

south

to birmingham

53 years ago

to a memory that is not of my life

but in my soul

to sunday morning

before church

when 4 mothers

braided bits of their hearts

twirled curls around fingers

tied ribbons

smoothed skirts

kissed forehead

with the same swelling of pride

as i had this morning

sent their 4 girls

bouncing and skipping

to worship

to praise

to hope

to love

sending them

to know god

without knowing

that evil

was going to send them

to see god's face

i'm sure they greased scalps

popped a fidgeting head

or 2

with the back of a comb or brush

i'm sure there were whispers of

don't get dirty

sit like a lady

mind your manners

tell so-and-so's mama i said hello

i'm sure those 4 girls

sat between their mother's knees

just as scarlett sat between mine

and complained that

a barrette was not her favorite

or that a ponytail was too tight

i don't know if they held hands

as they walked to church

or skipped in front of their mothers

but i know they were unknowingly

sent to their deaths

feeling loved

looking loved

being loved

i know their mothers

kissed a check

kissed a forehead

kissed with see you later

but it was good bye

today when homework is done

bellies are full

bodies are bathed

and as i tie silk scarves

around my daughters' hair

we will say their names

we send them our love

we will pray

we won't forget

I'm expected to wear my skin as a target, in shame and to apologize for it.

missing

to you

our daughters are things

to put your knees on

to snatch out of desks

to slam to the ground

to hang in cells

to execute in homes

to strangle over eyelashes

and murder over orange juice

our daughters are things

to watch on live feeds

being beaten and raped

and then have their pictures released

along with their names

because

to you

our daughters are things

16 thousand

missing black daughters

without outrage

without outcry

just, out of inventory

missing things to be replaced

because things are replaceable

and to you

our daughters are things

things to

objectify

appropriate

entertain

not to celebrate

to wear like a fashion trend

and toss off

crumple up

throw away

dead skin

to you our daughters are things

pre-existing conditions

i am

my daughters are

my sister is

my nieces are

my mother is

my girlfriends are

pre-existing conditions

say their names

who matters less than

black men dead in the streets

only the black women who weep

who matters less than our sons slain

only our bikini clad daughters

knees in their backs crying out in pain

who is muted more than our kings

only our slaughtered queens

say their names

#sandrabland #rekiaboyd #aiyannajones #miriamcarey
#yvettesmith #pearliegolden
#tarikawilson #shanteldavis #tyishamiller
#kathrynjohnston #jessicahampton

i am starting to lose track of their names
of their ages
of the streets and the states and the places
where badges pull triggers
on children
on babies
on niggers
they line up
like an infinite trail of sorrow
of mothers' tears
of fathers' anguish
from middle passage
'til today
where it's not safe for a boy child to play
if his skin brown
if his label black
standing perfectly still
is a threat an attack
riding in the passenger seat
feet far from the pedal
how was he in control?
how did he scare you?
as much as we hate you
cowards in blue

as much as we fear you

and the slaughter you do

as much as we want to rear up and fight

we teach our sons

hands up

be still

no flight

even then they wind up dead

and you and your uniform

will not be indicted

because our son's skin makes you

fear for your life

i am starting to lose track of their names

their eyes all look the same

their smiles whisper my son's name

they all look like my babies

all look like i carried them in my womb

in my heart

sons of my soul

you want me to lose track of their names

black boy die

black boy smart

black boy fly

black boy breathe

black boy die

black boy brilliant

black boy brash

black boy strong

black boy ash

black boy silent

black boy scream

black boy exist

no black boy dreams

black mother weep

black mother bent

black mother broken

hope and faith all spent

black mothers love

black mothers pray

black mothers plead

not my son today

magic

i am afraid that

my #blackgirlmagic is not enough

not enough to protect my son

my daughters

not enough to silence the sobs in my soul

**for mothers who consider arming their sons
when the rainbow of black murder by blue
uniforms is enough**

are you a mother?

do you have a son?

do you cry yourself to sleep at night worrying that every

year he ages, every day he gets closer to manhood

he is closer to being dead?

do you struggle with the fact that he is brilliant

and handsome

and tall

and funny

and joyful

and talented

and kind

and loving

and respectful

and watches out for his sister

makes his mother tea when she is sad

opens doors

pulls out chairs

that he knows what side of the street to walk on when

with a lady

that he gets amazing grades

that his teachers love him

that he can salsa and foxtrot

that he can hit a baseball out the park

that he loves comics

anime

and a girl named summer?

and none of that will protect him

you tell me what the fuck i can do to make sure he lives

tell me

life lessons

teach me
oh mighty white nation
how to tuck my son in bed
and not weep
how to not imagine his death
at the hands of those paid to protect him
teach me
with your righteous whiteness
how much education is enough protection
how much talent is enough of a shield
how much brilliance is enough to justify his
breath
i am begging
on my knees
praying to whatever god you say i should
what can i do to make your world
safe enough
for his life ?
how do i ensure that he will not be
a hashtag?
teach me
before my rage boils over

before he is a man
before his mother's tears fuel his vengeance
teach me
before my people
finally rise up
and strike down upon this nation
the terror you fear

bubba

yesterday my son turned 13

and by the eyes of the hate-filled people in this country

he is already a threat

he could live in a book

if i let him

live in anime, marvel, on tatooine, with hobbits

anywhere a story would lead

but i have to pull him out

watch the innocence drain from his eyes

teach him how to walk

hands out of pockets

hood off

that coming home alive

is worth the erosion of your dignity

teach him that his skin is a bull's eye

and tell him that because he is light

it won't be as bad as some of his friends

or as his own sister

because all i can arm him with is truth

his brilliance won't protect him

my love won't protect him

from the moment he exited my womb

a brown boy

he was targeted

as surely as pharaoh slaughtered sons

my son will be in the line of fire

to stop the next savior from

coming

you ask why are we angry

i ask

"what conversations have you had with your privileged

sons? "

have you had to tell him that this nation hates him

would kill him

then blame him

and walk over his body to the next

my anger is a righteous one

for the men i love

and the power i seek

to save my son!!

**you can't step
in our sons' blood,
serve us ice cream cones and
expect us not to hate you.**

no dmv

bubba said
i don't want a license
i don't want to drive
i don't want to get pulled over
49 times
i don't want to be shot
while my woman and baby watch
i think i'll just walk
in the daylight
ride my bike
roller skate
but even then i can't escape
breathing while black
standing while black
living while black
my mere existence
enough to make a pig
fear for his life
my living is a threat

am i next ?

dear young black men in these streets,

i love you.
i have looked into your eyes and i know
that you don't know
what love is
what it really feels like
to be wanted
safe
secure
to not be judged
to fly free and light
i see the targets
on your backs
drawn in brown skin
the moment you exit our wombs
i see you
soldier
locks swayin
red line ridin
i see you
and i need you
to dig down deep
into the reservoir of royalty

that you don't understand you have

i need you to be stronger

than you think you are already being

i need you

to look for god

and find him in your own reflection

because we need you

to be brave

to push past the barbed fences

that lock you in

lock you out

we need you to find a way

to fccl again

we need you to look on the faces

of dead babies

and feel again

i know feeling hurts

makes you think that it's weak

you can't afford to be weak

i know that the death that surrounds you

daily

numbs you

daily

apathy is

daily

'cuz survival is

daily

you call the boot on your neck

rahm

your father called it

daley

your grandfather called it

daley

either way

it holds you down

daily

suffocates you

daily

you are fighting

to breathe

daily

i know

we know

we still need you to become

the men that live inside you

that want to love

that want more than survival

that feel

when the blood
of babies flows endlessly
here in these streets
you are more than these streets
you don't own these streets
that's a lie they told you
so you could
die in these streets
a waste of your crown
rise up
we are waiting for you
the war is already here
the world has every right to fear
you
the earth quakes when you walk
rise up
fight for us
with us
we need you more than
the asphalt does
we need you to protect us
like you do your block
we are waiting with open arms
to catch you

embrace you

support you

we are waiting for you

to claim your kingdom

sincerely,

your mothers, sisters, aunties, ma'dears, nieces,

cousins, lovers, wives,

daughters...

...your queens

we are so magic that we skip
across waters
like light
cascading on
atlantic waves
with the prayers of
our ancestors whispering
in our ears from
watery graves

what does a bad dude look like ?

black

unarmed

not a threat

a 12 year old boy

a 18 year old boy

a 33 year old man

a man with a broken down car

hands in the air

selling movies

selling cigarettes

standing

breathing

living

sleeping

loving

working

taking a knee

running a country

my father

my brother

my son

what does a bad dude look like ?

and america answers...

america sings

america shouts

america pounds with blue bloody hands

black

black

black

black

black

black

black

black

black

black

a bad dude looks black

a bad dude looks dead

dead

dead

black dudes in america are dead

bad dudes

in our hoods

bad dudes

hide behind badges

bad dudes follow my

13 year old baby when he rides his skateboard

two blocks from our apartment

to buy candy from the gas station

at 10 am

on a saturday

bad dudes

pull men over

for nothing

rob them of the cash in their pockets

and send them on their way

angry and grateful to be alive

in our hoods

bad dudes tail you

'til your hands sweat

'til you fear

'til you forget to signal

right

then they have the right

to flash blue lights

and you'll swing in your cell

in our hoods

red white and blue

doesn't mean freedom

it means

you disappear in a warehouse

on the west side of chicago

and a gun is put down your throat

and your testicles are tasered

and your face is maced

and your family is threatened

'til you confess to crimes you didn't commit

and you go to 26th and cali

if you are lucky

if not

you just disappear

bad dudes pull you over

shoot you when your hands are up

because your car stalled

because you are a child with a toy gun

bad dudes burst into homes

kill women

shoot 5 year old babies

to serve a bench warrant

in my hoods

in my barrios

bad dudes often wear blue

my daddy said

let me tell you a secret

the police

were created during slavery

to uphold slavery

and after slavery

to control

free blacks

to keep them in line

to enforce black codes

to make sure

free wasn't free

to fill prisons

to continue to get free labor

and

enslave

black people

"when you make a good person enforce laws that are written with racist ink, even the best officer, filled with the upmost integrity, is upholding systemic racism." my daddy told me that

my daddy the cop

no fear

i'm not afraid of isis

unless isis shows up to my neighborhood

wearing blue

with a badge

because then their terror will be

legal

sanctioned

protected

celebrated

defended

and

wrapped in a stars and stripes bow

sins of the father

imagine if the value of your life was based upon the
morality of your parents.
if the sins they committed in youth,
in ignorance
in poverty
in the stank air of oppression
determined how high you could fly
how much you could dream
and if anyone could mourn your death
imagine your life
your chaos
your many ineptitudes
as the gage and the filter
people will judge your children with.
if every child was held accountable for the sins of their
parents
none of us would be exempt

dear joy lane,

this isn't your fault. you aren't responsible for evil. no more than the oppressed are responsible for the oppressor.

i hope you aren't reading what lost boys in men's clothing are writing. i hope you aren't listening. i hope it's not sinking into your soul like an osmosis of misogyny. i hope the stench of self-hating blackness isn't rotting so strong that your nose is filled with the putrid air of a broken people blaming you for brokenness.

sis i hope you know, that we know, this isn't because of you. that we know evil and mental illness aren't one and the same. i hope you know that we know what you mean when you say "he was a nice guy". the men who abused us were nice guys too.

joy, i hope our voices are louder, stronger, and more powerful than the screeching of hoteps, fuck boys, and the girls immune to their ignorance.

this wasn't your fault. there is no way for you to fix it. there was no way for you to prevent it. this wasn't your fault.

sincerely your sister in healing and love

leslé

protests

feet flooding streets

voices that organize can't weep

raised fists blacken sky

justice arrows

pull back

fly

lay on asphalt bed

civil unrest

die in

dead

profile protests

we are paris

we are belgium

we are never uganda

nigeria

kenya

tanzania

cameroon

palestine

haiti

and we are most definitely never

flint

or

chicago

terror compassion is color-coded more than the flags on

your profile pic

almost haiku

noose vs gun

hood vs badge

lynchings, are just televised now

my king

get yo' hands off my king

get yo' whitewashing

emasculating

rewriting history

lie-telling hands off my king

get yo' hands off his legacy

his words

our dream

get yo' hands off my king

get yo' misquoting

yo' paraphrasing

hiding a knife behind yo back

get yo' hands off my king

get yo' wiretappin'

bait-settin'

operative-trainin'

bomb-throwing

white hood-wearing

trump-voting

trigger-pulling

assassinating

hands off my king

he wasn't a pacifist
cheek-turning
boot-licking
"kneegrow"
he was a man-marching
blow-taking
suit-wearing
revolution-preaching
black woman-loving
black children-raising
king!
get his name out yo' mouth
no he is not rolling over in his grave
when we scream
black lives matter
when we flood the streets in protest
when we shut down your highways
and your stores on black fridays
when we organize and fight against
your pseudo-liberalism
that likes its "kneegrows"
quiet
calm
ball-dribbling

touchdown-making

joke-telling

shucking and jiving

he isn't rolling over

he's applauding

so get yo' hands off my king

freedom as a second skin

i don't have a selfie
with john lewis
i doubt if we've ever been
in the same room
or the same state
at the same time
but i stand with him
grateful to him
original freedom rider
freedom fighter
he's been crossing bridges
building bridges
burning bridges down
for longer than
most of us have been breathing
he's done more
in one day of his life
then a coon or a cheeto
will do in a lifetime
i stand with john lewis
sit with john lewis
kneel with john lewis

let his courage

wash over me

bless the scars

that tell the stories

of victories won

wars still fought

his life

his entire life

has been spent serving

waging equality's war

wielding diplomatic fists

with dignity of sacrifice

i stand with john lewis

proud and humble

fearless and resilient

he has bled for us

wearing freedom like a second skin

living legend

battle worn

we are forever indebted

forever i shall stand with him

4th

a long time a go, when my babies were young

they dressed in red white and blue.

we watched fireworks

they didn't ask questions

and i waited 'til they did.

now that they are old enough

to understand

to think

to articulate

we don't celebrate

we take a moment of silence

we mourn

we get angry

we create to release

we write

paint

dance

we grieve our ancestors who weren't liberated

on the 4th

in 1776

or 2016

if you ask them

my children will tell you

our people weren't free then

we aren't free now

ask my baby

her almost 8-year-old-lips will say

"the 4th of july isn't for my people. none of them"

"there is not a nation of the earth guilty of practices
more shocking and bloody than are the people of these
united states at this very hour"- frederick douglass
happy fourth of july america.

at least you are consistent.

golden niggers

the #gabbydouglas backlash

isn't backlash

it's america

and how america has always viewed

black people

dance nigger

sing nigger

cook and clean nigger

mammie my babies

tend to my life

entertain

and any glory you obtain

is because i have allowed it

smile nigger

happy nigger

be joyful when i beat you

rape you

kill you

don't complain nigger

don't aim too high nigger

i'll never let you forget

you ain't nothing but my nigger

pledge allegiance

to the flag

to hate

to oppression

to the foot on your neck

the knee in your back

the badge behind the barrel of a gun

don't slack nigger

'cause i'll take it all back nigger

every accolade

every acceptance you thought you had

they are all a mirage

i let you wear these stars and stripes

to cover your scars and stripes

so you can win me stars and hype

and gold

and you can invent

and discover

and create

and i shall appropriate

it all

and call

you

nigger

every chance i get

sincerely,

land of the free and the home of the slave

gold medal greatness

black girls

we so magic that we can fly

tumble and soar

with hundreds of years

of your knees in our backs

we leap

and spin

we land on 4 inches of wood

with the grace

we have learned from

the centuries of landing

on the lava of your hate

and not letting it burn

we so magic

that we skip across waters

like light cascading on atlantic waves

with the prayers of our ancestors whispering

in our ears from watery graves

we are so magic

that we will snatch the gold from your hands

that was pulled from the depths of our land

and toss it around our neck

before you have even touched the wall

before your feet touch

the ground

before the time stopped

before the score was set

before you realized you lost

we are so magic

that when you look at us

breaking the barriers you've built before us

you shudder

because you see the infinite black girl magic

behind us

before us

unbroken

unbent

black girls

we are so magic

#simones2016

no, will get you killed

i got a message.
from a dude i don't know
saying hello
i didn't reply
the messages continued
got angry
how dare i be so selfish
how dare i be such a bitch
to a soldier overseas fighting for my freedom
he must be in a wormhole
quantum leap
he's q from star trek
he's got a time turner
last time a war was fought for my freedom
the civil war
the battle of puebla
there is no current war
for my freedom
maybe a war for oil
or a war for american dominance
or funding wars of continued
palestinian oppression

but my freedoms are not threatened

by any nation other than my own

thank god he's just in my

inbox

and not grinding on me

shooting me when i say no

or

slicing my throat on a bus

when i say no

or

killing me and my baby

when i say no

to reconciliation

or

killing me when i say no

to an abortion

or

when i say no

to a proposal

or

when i say no

to giving him my number

or

when i say no

to giving him custody

or

when i say no

to him coming in my home

or

when i say no

to a train of soldiers

that i trained with,

raping me,

beating me,

killing me

and my government saying no

it didn't exist

and calling it a suicide

no can get you killed

if you are a woman

your manhood does not guarantee my submission

your desire is not my automatic yes

your uniform does not require me to say hello

your job does not give you authority over me

your fragile masculinity should not be

my death sentence

#toxicmen
#tiarahpoyau #janesetaltonjackson
#chericaadams #jessicahampton
#stephaniegoodloe #maryspears
#nokuthulathashe #kasandraperkins
#apriljace #lavenajohnson

uncle joe

i had an uncle joe
who by all accounts was
gentle
kind
funny
all i have from him
are blurry memories
that all were mostly gifts
from others' minds
i had an uncle joe
who worked at a general store as a teen
told the white owner
to kiss his ass
after she called him a nigger
i had an uncle joe
whose mouth
made the klan come for his family
so his family left mississippi
in the middle of the night
in a model-t ford
headed back to new orleans
with joe still alive

i had an uncle joe

who distanced himself from his family

separated to spare us

the shame of him

the shame of

a catholic black gay man

he took his life

after decades long isolation

an isolation to save his family

the shame

of watching him die

my father

who i have never thought of as liberal

or progressive

would decimate you

if you used the f word

would explain to you

the difference between choice

and birth

a gay rights activist

without trying

without going to a march

just by

loving his brother

missing his brother

his only brother

when we talk of his brother

he says

hate killed joe

hate and ignorance

he laments the years of separation

remembers the years

where the world was colder

hates the empty space

his only brother

left in his heart

an uncle joe-sized space

the space where love

removed itself from love

to spare love the humiliation

to spare love from being ostracized

to spare love the pain of the world's

judgement

i can not imagine

the loneliness

of a southern catholic gay black man

in 1960

how he must have looked for safety

from his skin

from his heart

from his family

because catholic white gods don't mix

with homosexuality

unless it's behind closed doors

locked in vatican vaults

jim crow and homophobia

strolled american streets

back then

hand in hand

skipping on bible belt roads

lovers who gave birth to

tea party

trump voting

bigoted

xenophobic

mobs

who could they possibly hate more than

a gay black man ?

i had an uncle joe

who was my father's only brother

his older brother

my grandmother's

favorite

the first honoré boy to survive

the tragedies of infancy

and

southern poverty

which were always a looming death threat

i had an uncle joe

by all accounts

he was kind

funny

laughed loudly

gave generously

and bravely carved out his own truth

in the face of a world

that told him

everything about him was unwanted

unworthy

unloved

i had an uncle joe

state aid

who mourns the friendless
the homeless
the hopeless
the helpless
who says prayers
with names on their lips
of lives that have gone
unspoken
forgotten
who smells the stench of soul aches
more putrid than heartbreaks
who will love for love's sake
who will mourn the toe tags
in body bags that go unclaimed
who will mourn the lost
who only own their names
who will bury the vessels
and not render them depraved
who will shovel the dirt
when the state won't pay for a grave

rainbow connections

america breeds a special kind of hate

a violent

entitled

vile

kind of hate

it has nothing to do with islam

everything to do with this country

it's guns

it's christian right

it's genocide

it's slavery

it's oppression

this nation's womb gives birth to hate babies

filled with fear

false feelings of superiority

nurses them

on propaganda pus-filled breasts

rocks them with super power hands

educates them with gop ignorance

and they grow into 3/5 of a soul

labeling the world 3/5 human

and the soulless don't care about

voiceless babies being slaughtered

or brown boys executed in the streets

or women raped by dumpsters

or sanctuaries of music, solidarity and safety

for persecuted rainbows.

dear matt lauer,
there is no irony in ali changing his name from clay to
muhammad, because clay was a famous abolitionist.
the irony is that, though you claim ali to be your
"personal hero", your privilege does not allow you to
understand why he would not want the name clay.
regardless of who that man was.
for a people without a name. without a land. without a
language. without a god that wasn't forced upon them at
the other end of a

whip

noose

fire hose

dog

pig

legislation

our right to define ourselves without your fucking
approval is what we desire.
even in his death, you still question your "hero's" logic
behind changing his name !!!
his name !
you, and people like you, are still putting him a box,
that now, because he is no longer with us, he cannot
escape.
if he could speak, he would have told you that you are
an oppressor. he would have screamed it in your face.
we can't have shit.

not our culture that we have created

not our heroes

nor even our names

#ourgoat
#kuntanottobe
#muhammadalinotcassiusclay

ali

do not attempt to sanitize

whitewash

misrepresent

tarnish

say he transcended race

idolize what you don't understand

he will always be ours

always

unapologetically

black

muslim

man

all the things that makes this nation tremble

you loved him after parkinson's silenced him

we loved him fighting

growing

jailed

winning

losing

f.o.i and sunni

he was not a just a boxer

he was...

revolution personified

freedom forged in brown fists

he was ours

#goat

rinse and repeat

we publicize

go live

record

report

our pain

our blood flowing like rivers

and it makes no difference

killers will be

indicted

never convicted

blue freedom

over

black lives

repetitively

black death the new groundhog day

for st. louis

i am not sure what you want from us

our silence

or our death

our bodies as commodities

or as target practice

our hairstyles for costumes

or for condemnation

our skin to wear

when the bronzer runs out

like latex on your soul

impenetrable by justice

or conscience

you want us to

run and catch and fetch and step

but not to kneel

to dance and sing and act and heal

but not to scream

to build and dream and innovate

but not to demand

to water the pavement with our blood

but not to protest on the streets

to exist

for consumption
for entertainment
for lust
but to do it invisibly
not to be seen or heard or valued
to be used and killed and forgotten
for we aren't human
less than 3/5
our mothers are not allowed
to mourn our deaths
our fathers (if you let them live)
are not allowed righteous rage
we are not allowed the justice
you bestow on a dead dog
because we are just magic
that you can pull out of a hat
pull out of a car
pull out of a freezer
pull out of a home
pull out of a land
pull out of a god
pull out your whip
pull out your dick
pull out your noose

pull out your guns

and fire

5 shots

16 shots

lorraine motel

shots

but we should not

cry out in pain

in loss

in rage

in hope

lest you remind us

with slander

with tear gas

with riot gear

with handcuffs

with jail cell suicide

with the albatross of felonies

with constant reminders

of our lack of humanity

in your courts

forever blind to the inequities

heaped upon

skin with melanin

#justiceforanthonysmith

FIRE

new love

like an incandescent kiss on my face when the sun
finally breaks from behind the cloud
that's how his love spreads across my soul
warm. reassuring. life giving after endless cloudy days.

midnight musings

he be to me
what bass be to rhythm
what blend be to harmony
he the smell of fresh air after rain
he who sounds like angels singing whenever he says my
name
he who gives clichés depth
making even the asinine profound to me
he be my amazing grace
for once i was blind
but now all is see is he

church

he parts with his tongue
to part with his tongue
parts that come undone
from the inside out
his fingertips leave finger prints
of ownership
all over my flesh
claiming time
space
and place
his kingdom
his domain
where he has absolute reign
breath be kept
quick and fast
making climax last
like tantric
hours at a time
going past physical
through cerebral
enters mind
dives into soul

filling abandoned holes

making me whole

whispering sweet some things

not void promises

but vows

blest

time with him is sacred

sabbath

he is church

sanctuary

no less

his leg

the weight of his leg

across me

early morning reminder

saying

i belong in this space

seas of sheets

magic had

to be remade

the weight of his leg

warm on my thigh

heavy with love

saying

i am his

staking claim

claim to my heart

my body

my soul

every inch of sinew

flesh and bone

spirit and tendon

marrow and blood

belong to him

the weight of his leg

holding me down

holding us down

under him i am

protected

under him i am

fearless

under him i am

all that i was created to be

the weight of his leg

marks passion had

warm sweat

echoes of satisfied moans

his legs across me

i sleep

he watches

he sleeps

i move

inching toward

him

hip rotation

leg above

me below

he

inside

his legs

across me

my legs

around him

it says

i am now whole

friday night haiku for you

paint me with your tongue
kiss color into my flesh
tattoos of climax

morning quickie

back arches
legs tremble
breath soft sigh
fingers reaching
bottom lip bitten
eyes rollin back
slow
hips roll
nipples harden
mouth opens
tongue moistens
delirious delight

after hours, grown folks, late night edition

you... the curve in my lips
open invitation
for soul communication
arch giver
sweat enhancer
each moan
full of you
trembles in thighs
throaty pleasure filled sighs
hypnotic hip rhythms in the ride
your entire soul finds solace inside
call my pussy home
warm hands
spread cross back
spread cross heart
spread cross part
legs east to west
perfect lack of rest
sleepless nights mean
fingers in hair
fist full
moving head to head

on bed

hand prints

ass red

infinite the explorations

without prude limitations

in other words...

i love how you fuck me

time with him is sacred
sabbath
he is church
santuary
no less

showers

let your hands guide themselves
like fingers over braille
water over skin
let them glide
over each curve
tuck themselves into valleys
memorize the places that
make me shudder
bite my lower lip
moan slowly
imprint hands on hips
lips
thighs
cover me with your hands
'til the water turns cold
and my skin is hot

fall into me

be engulfed

sink into sweet folds of flesh

be entwined

legs and arms

tendon and sinew

be exalted

sacred moans

hymns of pleasure

tongues that speak silently

worship whispered in your ear

let me kneel before you

in reverence

my only prayer to please you

drench me

baptize me

let me be born anew

wet with your satisfaction

fall into me

you

you seep into my cells
desire's osmosis
you
memory
fantasy
unfamiliar comfort
a paradox
fear
anticipation
addiction
obsession
even the withdrawal is ecstasy
evidence of your touch
te extraño

missing you

quickly with you is not enough
it's like a fleeting summer
a warm breeze gone before
it brushes against my skin
a sunset that dips
beneath clouds before i can
exhale
in appreciation
quickly with you is torture
you like wine on my tongue
savored and sweet
inhaled like a prayer of thanksgiving
grateful to be drunk
with the joy of you
you like mornings on
sunday
warm sheets
cool pillow
quiet moans
you like time infinite
my rebirth my renewal
you the epitome of hope

none of which comes quickly

quickly with you is oxymoronic

i want forever to lose myself in your caress

a millennium to melt in your arms

even a lifetime of love making

seems insufficient

i want to watch the world end and be reborn again

with you inside me

feel the explosions of new universes

with your climax

feel the shudders of new civilizations

with the trembles of my thighs

arch my back into eternity

and feel you penetrate into

creation itself

quickly with you is a drop of water

i crave your ocean

tongue moistens
delirious delight

'til

i am going to love you
'til the bad thoughts
disappear
and the tears
are no longer an option
and there is nothing but
yes
on your lips

haiku 12.13.14

we are eternal
space can't separate my love
our souls tied always

haiku for you

the ghost of your touch
anticipation's shadow
longing etched inside

girdles

loving you is
like wearing a stretched out girdle
i put you on
but i barely feel you there
you are supposed to help me hold in
all of life's rolls
instead you just roll down
i need to take you off

give her my number

i have tattooed myself into your spirit
etched myself into your soul
echoes of my moans
forever in your ears
i'm always in your hair
you will hear my laughter in every song
taste my lips every time you eat
i am so entwined into your dna
that if someone wants to learn you
they will have to know me first

berry

i liked giving myself away to you
wrapping pieces of my love
in delicate tissue paper
placing them in ornate boxes
with intricate bows
putting those boxes in your
large brown denzel hands
strong and smooth
scarred and sweet
perfect even with crooked pinkies
and shadows of stitches
from broken bones
i laid my heart in your lap
for the first time
i wasn't ashamed
to let someone see it
to see the places it was broken
to see the sloppy repair work
to peer at the patches
to look at my clumsy attempts to fix it
alone
without tools

just with hope and prayers

i treated you to...

the laughter and love of my children

which is magic not of this world

the respect of my father

which i still crave endlessly

the tenderness of my mother

abundant and rare

inclusion from

my sister

niece

brother

friends

i offered them all on a platter

to share

to replenish

to strengthen

i have found

in your absence

that the love i gave away

isn't gone

i am not depleted

nor do i regret

i liked giving myself away to you

watching you unwrap me

discover me

revel in the fantasies i made real

looking at myself

through your eyes

thinking

what an amazing gift he has

then the epiphany

the amazing gift

is

me

i am

fucking

amazing

living through you

learning

how to love me

i discovered

how to love myself

i thank you for that

creep

i have waited for you

soul naked

body wrapped in sheets

with sunset glowing in my hair

in countless hotels

littered across

concrete tangled intersections

road maps

landmarks

junctions

leading to nowhere

in particular

waiting to open myself

flay body

provide passage

into the universe

into power and solace

energy and respite

into life

hand on back

beckoning to burdens unspoken

lay them in my lap

for my strength is infinite

hand on heart

pleading between pleasure and pain

for my love heals

waiting willingly willfully whispering

to your soul

i want you to notice when i'm not around

*i discovered
how to love myself
i thank you for that*

f.i.b.

being strong

is so fucking heavy

i can't fall apart

i can't give up

i can't decide

not to decide

being strong

all the time

is too heavy

to lift

every day

and then you came along

with

strong hands

and broad shoulders

and tender eyes

and lips that kissed

with love

and promises

you told me

i could lean on you

stand in the sun with you

breathe easier

trust

and then you left

the burnham

i wonder if you knew

that the last time

was the last time

if your hands knew

they were saying good bye

did you tell your hips

that a cold night at the end of february would be their

last dance with me

their last moments of being engulfed

in the softness of my

inner most inner most

the closest to heaven that they will ever be

i wonder if you told them

did your back try to remember

the trace of my fingers

the scratch of my nails

did your lips know

to drink the curve of my neck

for more than just my pleasure

but to etch the memory in your soul

did you bury your face

and linger in my hair

to breathe deep

to

fill your lungs with the scent of me

fill your spirit with the scent of me

fill your heart with the scent of me

do you still search for the source

of my sillage

like a shadow of joy in your life

do my moans echo in your ears

wake you before the sun

does your body ache for me

like an amputated limb

ghost pain

does the memory of perfection

punch you like ali

in the gut

does the absence of me

feel like january chicago wind

on your face

do you long for my sun

do you know

you must know

i will never return with summer

viejo

i long for the way my body
curved to meet yours
the electric feel of your hands
on my skin
the warmth of your kiss
that radiated far from my lips
reached into my soul
and birthed a new me
and now that it is gone
i search for duplications
or satisfaction
and they are all hollow
empty
not even a shadow of you
faint whisper of pleasure
like trying to catch
fog

13

gonna take all the poems i wrote you

the ones you read

the ones you never will

the ones i cried on

the ones jealousy fed to fires

the ones i scream in

the ones i hate you in

the ones with blood for ink

seeped in pages of pain

gratitude

joy

memories i wish weren't in the past

the ones full of foolish faith

all consuming hope

the love poems

all the fucking love poems

tear them up

toss them in the air like glitter

swallow and shoot them out my ass

like lactose intolerant gas

i am allergic to being loved and left

having to act like an adult

like a well-behaved adult

when i want to cut you

watch you gasp for breath

like i do at night

when the pain of missing you

wraps round my body

like a cop's chokehold

around a black man's neck

i want your all

or

nothing

friendship is a watered down insult

to our passion

i don't put water in my tequila

i don't water down my life

i am not a cheap shot

i'm a field of agave

i am petty

queen of grudges

i wish you pain

useless pain

that you gave to yourself

in the name of love

and honor

and integrity

and self-preservation

and the useless chivalry of protecting me

from you

ashes to ashes

dust to weak dicks

growing and ghosting

growth comes

when you no longer

hope to build your life in him

in his arms

in his lips

in the scent of him that lingers

on your skin

growth comes

when you know

that you

are the foundation

the air

earth

water

fire

that someone is dreaming

of building his life with

growth comes

when you no longer beg

for what no longer wants you

when you hold the phone

but do not call

when you hold the pen

and write only good byes

growth comes

when you remember

a man will pursue what he wants

he will make a way

out of no way

he will build bridges in the air

he will stop at nothing

when he sees his destiny

growth comes from knowing

flowers don't fly to the bees

growth comes from

longing to be loved

and no longer

longing for his love

it comes when you can appreciate

2 years of perfection

and not drown in losing

a lifetime of joy

it comes when the entire day has passed

rise to set

and you have not wept

or curled into moments

hibernating in memories

when you rest your body

and have not thought of him

even to acknowledge

that you have not thought of him

growth comes

when you can admit

that all of the above is bullshit

lies you tell yourself

to function

to breathe

to not disintegrate into the abyss

the way his love did

the third

i understand why you are angry
if i was loved by me
knowing how i love
and then could no longer be loved by me
i'd be angry too
if i had walked out on me
i would also be ashamed
and i would tell people we separated
as if it was mutual
to hide the fact
that
i took me for granted
if i had been an idiot
and thought that after hurting me
i could come back to me
and me was like
"nah"
i'd be throwing hissy fits too
i'm not saying that i excuse your behavior
or that i forgive you
or that i want to share air with you
ever

again

i'm just saying i understand

me is pretty fucking fabulous

i'd be pissed if i fucked up with me too

#horchata

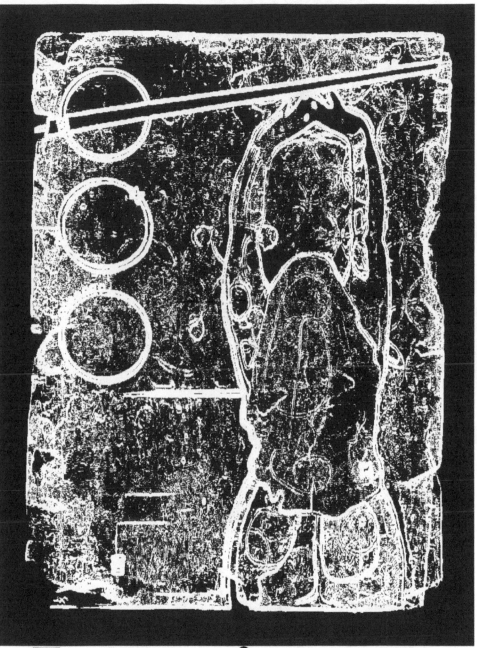

Lagniappe

dearest, i can't help you love black people.

this is not your experience.

you are not from what has made them

you come from freedom.

your lineage was not broken under slavery.

your ancestors were free

your dna doesn't not know this pain

it's not about education

or lack there of

this is my family

all of them

the ghetto and the graduate

the lost and the successful

the ones who hate my light skin

and the ones who wrongfully glorify it

the ones who think we should pull ourselves up from

our boot straps

the ones who know the bootstrap is an illusion

the project and the mansion

the president and the drug dealer

the activist and gangbanger

i love them

even when they don't love me

understand me

see me

accept me

and i see their beauty

especially when they don't see their own

i simply love my people

my family

my kinfolk

with collective pain and collective barriers that some
overcome just to learn there are more hills to climb
more battles to fight,
i mourn and weep for us

i will fight for us

i can't make you love us

understand us

you don't consider yourself us

and darling that's ok

just don't expect us to always consider you

even though we do

even though we long to bring you into the fold

to wrap you in the soul of a people who have been
persecuted more than any other people on the planet
and still love
hard and deep and strong

you are stuck in a hurt that a teenager experienced

and you have carried it into your adulthood

i can't change that

fix it

heal it

you have made your own life

live it

surrounded by whatever and whomever you feel
solidarity with
and that's ok
but know that voice that whispers

"why don't they love me, understand me?"

that voice that made you reach out to me

that is the voice of your family

who longs to love you

and be loved by you in return

with peace and love,

leslé

dear diallo
these past weeks i've been on edge.

weepy. angry. sad.

i've sat in the sun with people i love. danced 'til my feet
hurt. laughed and sang almost every day, trying to
shake off the sadness that wraps me like a heavy
blanket the moment i am alone. i knew today was
coming. and no matter how much i tried i couldn't stop
it.

today it's 4 years without you. my friend. my light. the
smile that beckoned broken souls to come nearer and
be loved. the whisper and gentle push to a very young
me, to stand in my own light. to write. and be received.

your love echoes loudly still. i try to recreate the joy you
gave freely. i write ceaselessly words i know you will
never read.

to say i miss you is hollow. the night sky misses the
stars if they were to disappear. the scorched earth
would miss the rain that never would return. and you
were that to me. a light in the darkness. cool calm
tenderness to scars that were still hot to the touch.

my soul aches. it laments. it screams in silence that the
world is void of you. sometimes the days are so dark
without your spirit. you were brilliance. radiance. peace.
and i still can not believe you are gone.

i love you diallo. always

dear don (sellout is too nice a name for you) lemon,

no martin would not be rolling over in his grave about baltimore burning. he would be weeping that 50 years later, we still believe that a system created to suppress, oppress and destroy us, would ever protect and support us.

it's revolution when egyptians do it, bravery in tiananmen square, necessary for walls crumbling in berlin and just fun when white college students do it... but let us revolt in anger of the continuous murder of our people... we are no better than animals

#fuckyoulemon

sally speaks

i cannot be your mistress

and your slave

i can't be your lover

if you own me

from birth to grave

that wasn't my room

adjacent to his

it was my cell

for quick access for his pleasure

and my hell

i can't consent

while being owned

i can't say yes

if i'm not allowed a no

i was born from rape

i was born to be raped

and to birth after rape

i was not woman

i was thing

possession

chattel

inventory

soulless

3/5

a price on a ledger

breeder

exploited

exotic

alone

captive

dead before death

not even my breath belonged to me

the slave has no agency

did it arouse your founding father

when i wept

when i screamed

when from pain i bore beige babies

that would never collect

their inheritance

but were left denied

forgotten

trash from my womb

reminders of your perversion

the abomination of you wanting me

i can't be

your mistress

and your slave

i bear witness

from cradle to grave

and i hold these truths to be self-evident

that all founding fathers were created

evil

dear officer,

we don't need you

to jump rope

or hand out chips

we don't need you to do

running man challenges

or play a game of pick up

we need you tell check your partner

before he stops to reload

after having emptied

16 shots into a boy

we need you to have the courage

to break code of silence

to intervene

to call out the injustice

that you know you are subject to

when your blue uniform is no longer

on your black skin

we need you to not defend

or cover up

and hide

bloody blue hands

we need a revolution from within

not your continued complacency

we need you to not put your badge

before your conscious

we know you are not all corrupt

can you admit

that we are not all criminals ?

as you don't want to be judged by the

heinous actions of a few of your brethren

trump hands

(an open letter to mothers of little girls who are triggered when watching trump molest)

when sage was 6, one of her closest friends had a party at american girl place.

14 little black girls showed up in a limo, beautiful dresses, shiny shoes, ruffled socks, big bows in their hair. like god had dropped little angels on chicago and michigan ave.

they pranced in the store, giggling with their friends, shopping for their dolls, no different than the 100 plus other girls dressed up and happy, except they were black. all of them. and their mamas were too.

they sat at the largest table in the cafe. and were catered to, like the other girls there, eating and celebrating, except they were black.

i dance to the rhythm of racial ambiguity around midwestern white people, because sage is a stunning milk chocolate brown, people often don't think she's my daughter. even though we look ridiculously alike.

i heard things that day. things i know were said because these girls were black.

i heard things when i lagged behind the group, things like

"i've never seen such cute ones."

"i just want to pet them"

"i'm gonna take their pictures"

many times, when i've walked downtown with my children, random people have touched their curls. reached to caress their skin. complemented me on "dressing" them so well.

when i watched trump grab that beautiful girl. kiss her as she pulled away. heard him complement her parents on the great job they were doing because she was pretty (what else could he be judging, not knowing her at all) it took me back to that day at american girl. watching people ogle at our daughters because they were lovely and well behaved. because for some disgusting reason, that is not the expectation.

understanding that their objectification began then and there. their value based on their beauty and that any privileged person felt they had a right to access it. to touch it. pet it. hold it. kiss it.

because what are they but black girls, born to black men and women and we all know how valued we are, right ?

as a mother to black and brown children, the pain is constant. it is an ache that my son will be considered a man and a threat before he even knows what manhood is. and my daughters will be objectified, sexualized and demeaned because this country actually has a presidential candidate that feels he can grab them by the pussy.

love letter to the land known as america,
today when the nation celebrates your rapist, the
figurehead that symbolizes the genocide that followed
after his ships.

the ships that danced on an ocean with death and
destruction like wind in the sails of the nina, the pinta
and the santa maria.

today while parades are thrown in his honor ... your
children, your descendants the ones that were here,
brown like the land, before it was discovered, and the
children you adopted after they were stolen and forced
to pour their blood and tears into your soil, we shall
mourn for you.

we love you. broken. and scarred.

we will light candles

remember our ancestors

tell our children truths not in your books

we will remind them, that although the face of america
is capitalism, greed, bigotry, misogyny, entitlement and
hate, personified in the being of trump...

...this land is our land
this land is my land
from california to the new york island
from the redwood forest to the gulf stream waters
this land was made by you and me

sincerely,
daughter of the indigenous and descendant of the
enslaved

dear amy schumer and leah dunham,
your whiteness does not entitle you to the attention and
or affection from odell or any other black man.

much like the myth of big foot or the loch ness
monster... the myth of pasty, pudgy-faced white women
being the epitome of beauty and the ultimate desire of
all black men, simply isn't true.

it is a lie you tell yourself to make your blandness feel

superior.

stop.

santa isn't real

the easter bunny isn't real

and neither is your deemed importance

dear 2016,
i hate you more than i hate my ex

more than i hate bad gumbo
more than i hate spineless school principals
more than i hate gov. rauner
more than i hate darth susans

more than i hate slum lords, parking tickets, bad
breath, bad kissers, people who touch my children's
hair without permission, catcallers who harass my
teenager, bad music, micro-aggressions, pretentious
tacos, vegan cheese, and gum poppers.

rest in laughter gene wilder. thank you for the joy you
gave. thank you especially for some of the best comedic
one liners ever, but thank you for 2 specific movie
memories.

1. watching young frankenstein with my parents and
watching them laugh 'til they cried. 'til they held their
stomachs. 'til they had to catch their breath. 'til my
mom was red in the face. 'til my father looked at her
and then at my children and then me, and told us about
their first date. going to see it. laughing with her. seeing
his eyes travel back in time.

2. thank you for willie wonka. thank you for

"candy is dandy but liquor is quicker"

"i said good day sir"

for a land of pure imagination.
for every wild eyed and mischievous grin.
and a soft voice that followed like chocolate rivers.

2016... you just keep taking, don't you
#ripgenewilder

dear "she was asking for it"

agency

autonomy

the ability to proudly say yes

and to say no

when you slut shame

you contribute to rape culture

if i'm not worthy to be a whole sexual being by my own

choices then of course i can't deny you.

when i'm

drunk

unconscious

or just don't want you

this is how sexism works.

men are allowed to sexually explore.

to be satisfied

and seek satisfaction

without shame

women are not

we can not be openly sexual without shame

we can not be violated without blame

this society tells us we do not have the agency over our

bodies

our sexuality

it belongs to men

who can take it, if they want, and face little to no

consequences

because we were asking for it

we wore short skirts

we went to a party

we were fast

we wanted a promotion

a raise

to leave you

are sex workers

walked down the street alone

our mother is dating you

we danced provocatively

we are worth less than a man

so we should just shut up when we are attacked

because we don't own our own bodies

anyway, right?

love liberates

i hope my love

gives my babies wings

wings so strong

so wide

that when they spread them

they eclipse the sun

i hope my love sends them soaring

past earthly blue skies

into galaxies

so they can run their fingers

through the stardust of

dreams fulfilled

i hope my love liberates

catcaller

catcaller: what dat mouth do

me: talk shit

catcaller: what dat pussy taste like

me: my pussy tastes like justice...

my pussy tastes like justice

like revolution rolled into cinnamon dipped

honey-mango-coated sweetness

to help you swallow bitter black hate

my pussy tastes like power purpose and peace

my pussy tastes like knowledge and passion

universe-flavored

seasoned with stardust

my pussy tastes like infinity

she is alpha and omega

the beginning and the end

my pussy tastes like genesis

it leads

it rules

even her whispers are shouts

my pussy tastes like command

inspiration and integrity

a compass for more than your phallus

my pussy directs your soul

my pussy tastes like queendom come

when i come

my reign makes it rain

hot sweet sticky

my pussy tastes better than mediocre men's tears

my pussy tastes like

matriarchal militias

mutating by millions

marching heavy on your tongue

my pussy tastes like justice

for #2
with love,
#4
if you are lucky

you will have someone

in your life

who will blow on your embers

they won't let your flame be extinguished

not if the heavens monsoon on it

not if gale force winds swirl around it

not if the love of your life pisses on it

not even if you

in your size 10s

try to stamp it out

because you are weary

because the fight has drained you

because the darkness hovers

always close

always breathing on your neck

threatening to swallow you whole

as if you carry *the nothing* on your back

like a decorative piece of luggage

if you are lucky

you will find someone who

stands in the rain

faces the storm

and lends you hope

to close the canyons

wide and empty

black holes of isolation and pain

they will speak life

breathe on your embers

that you have crushed into ash

because of fear

because of hopelessness

they will keep your fire going

when you can't even find the pit

they will speak life to your soul

they will remind you of who you are

of who you have always been

remind you that

not only is your fire

everlasting

it is in you

in the pit of your belly

in the lining of your soul

you open your mouth

and spit fire

because you are a fucking dragon

they will shout into your cave

where you lay curled and quiet

like some myth

some bedtime story

dormant

harmless

forgotten

they will come

and scream

"wake your ass up and come burn this bull shit down"

if you are lucky

you will find someone who

breathes life onto your embers

they will not let you settle into ash

if you are lucky

if you are lucky

and if not

you must learn to stoke

your own damn flame

brown girl,
brown girl,
how are you so strong?
'cause I got queens
in my blood
pushing me along

"our destiny is not written for us but by us" -obama

i see you
the you inside the pretty
inside the smile
inside the worry
inside the wanting
to make the wrongs
rights

i see the parts that are afraid
to say the wrong thing
do the wrong thing
be the wrong thing

i see the shoulders rise
and the doubts rise
and the fear rise
and you fight to take a deeper breath
to tilt your head a little higher
and walk on

i see you
the real you
past the hurt you
the timid you
 the little you

i see you
beautiful and brilliant
proud and regal
crowned and glorious
purposeful and graceful
smart and strong
i see you woman
i see you godchild
i see you niece
i see you
destiny

if you ever can't see yourself
if you ever doubt too long
if the lies other mouths whisper get too loud

i will help you
remember you
because i see you

depression is a sad dance partner

he doesn't care that my feet hurt
that i am tired
that i don't like the song
that i don't know the steps
that it's late
that i want to go home
he drags me on the floor
holds me too close
steps on my toes
breathes in my face
sways with me limp in his arms
long after the music stops

i promise to not spend the next
50 or more years hating you,
reminiscing on
youth long gone,
but to be grateful
for every day I have you,
my body

kanye misses the old kanye too

society standards for being sane

are unachievable

especially for black and brown people

the expectation is that our magic

is supposed to suppress

stress

depression

anger

loss

grief

we are not supposed to feel

we are supposed to endure

entertain

enlighten

evoke

we are only to be enjoyed

don't break

don't hurt

don't look into the abyss

and fall in head first

don't scream out loud

when you keep falling

but never seem to touch the ground

don't be real

don't do it on a stage

don't do it on camera

don't break

i've lost myself to darkness before

sometimes i still stand with my toes

draping over the cliff of bottomless pain

i know what crazy tastes like

its bitterness coats your tongue

aftertaste like aspartame

lingering toxicity

i know what the weight of depression

feels like

hitting your soul

like meteors hit earth

leaving craters behind

fighting to return to light

is beyond hard

it is real

it is not all in our heads

thank god my break didn't happen with

a mic in my hand

i'm sure kanye misses the old kanye too

bubba got into a fight today

he said i was in gym
these dudes kept sayin
gay jokes
it pissed me off
and i told them
they were idiots
and ignorant
and should get that stupid shit
away from me
my friend could hear them
and she was crying
'cuz she's gay
and i was pissed mom
really pissed
and i told them to shut up
he got in my face
said my friend was going to hell
she shouldn't be allowed near us
she was evil
so i shoved him
and we fought
i'm sorry

he looked for my reaction
"are you mad at me ?"
for not letting assholes spew hate
for being angry and hurt
for standing up for a friend
for being the young man
i expect you to be
never mad
he smiled
i asked if his friend was ok
if he was hungry
and we rode home happy
bubba got into a fight today
and i couldn't be prouder

dear "how you gonna cry over white carrie fisher and not the hundreds of murdered black people in the streets of chicago" and all other hotepians ,

first, the character of princess leia and general organa was a bad ass. she wasn't given anything. she lost everything. her parents. her planet. her brother. her son. her love. and she still showed up. she fought. she led. the empire is what is in office now. may all of our princesses show up, on the front lines and kick ass. we are not just pretty bikini-clad slaves. we are generals, leading a rebellion.

carrier fisher, the woman was more than our leia. she was an author, a screenwriter and a survivor. she fought mental illness and it's stigma. she was hollywood royalty and used that platform to shed light on darkness.

she was a giver of no fucks.
taker of no shits.

she didn't hide behind her mistakes in loathing pity. she weaponized them. she wore them like jewelry as if to say "look at what i have conquered, look at what i have survived".

i am mourning her and taking up her mantle at the same time.

i can love my people. weep for them. fight for them and still find a piece of my soul that can honor another life as it transitions, even if her shell does not look like my own.

if i only love what is reflective of my dna,
do i not become what i hate ?

the rebellion has my back

come for me if you want.
you've been warned.

my brother was a jedi

my father was the chosen one.

he wielded both dark and light.

he balanced the force with the sacrifice of his life

i have a blaster in my hand

and the rebellion has my back

come for me if you want...

just know the force is strong with this one

#iamgeneralorgana

my black boy doesn't play ball

doesn't dribble or dunk

but he's tall

likes comics and dance

doesn't sag his pants

my black boy doesn't play ball

my black boy doesn't like his dad

he's caught between disappointment

and mad

he looked for a king

found deferred dreams

my black boy doesn't play ball

my black boy has a brown mom

makes her smile with jokes and some songs

he takes out the trash

shovels snow for some cash

for her he tries to be strong

my black boy is growing into a man

every day a bit taller he stands

i don't fear the streets

but the pressures he'll meet

as he fights this world

with black hands

my black boy is radiant joy

i fight so this world won't destroy

his light or his laugh

as he blazes manhood's path

no longer my curly haired boy

manage it

it's quiet without the kids
break is over
endless fights are done
bags packed
lunches made
edges fleeked
christmas' jordans pristine
and now the house is silent
it's quiet without the kids
it's a temporary peace
that is both relished and rejected
the afternoon will return chaos
i do my best work in chaos
pressure is like a pep rally
like a double dog dare
"manage this" it screams...
too little money
overeducated
underpaid
be 3 different mothers
to 3 different people
with 3 different souls

an ex who thinks

10 min car rides to school

is fatherhood

10 min rides are enough time

to parent

a biological uber

who thinks we should clap

for fish who swim

manage always having

to take the high road

you can't fold

you can't lose it

you can't dive into the seduction of depression

and it's beautiful warm land of

nothing

manage bigotry's dementors

gliding behind brown babies

shadows of the world's hate

whispering patronous prayers

filling your seeds with magic

hoping it's enough

manage making a boy into a man

girls into women

artists into activists

help their brilliance turn into

quasars

"manage it" pressure screams at me

pour yourself into them

but save enough of yourself, for yourself

be a mama

but be a milf

be smart

but be funny

be sexy

but not kim k

be an activist

but say it quietly

be bold

but not brash

be a boss

not a bitch

be independent

but not so much that it's intimidating

be a friend

but walk away from toxicity

be a walking breathing contradiction

be a beautiful paradox

a delicate flower that will kill

"manage it" pressure screams

bark like a dog

hop on one foot

catch all life throws

make the lemonade

turn the frown upside down

be the clichés

only the good ones of course

don't be a stereotype

even though

on paper

you are one

brown single mama

manage it

smile while you do it

enjoy the quiet without the kids

but love the cacophony too

pressure is a loud-talkin

gum-poppin

bitch

and i manage her daily

brown girl, brown girl

what do you see
i see a world that thinks
it's better than me
brown girl, brown girl
what do you do
i paint, run and sing
and sometimes i flew
brown girl, brown girl
what do you know
that sometimes my skinfolk
don't want me to grow
brown girl, brown girl
what do you feel
that it takes more than magic
to help all of us heal
brown girl, brown girl
what do you see
a world that sees my skin
before it sees me
brown girl, brown girl
whatcha gonna do
march, fight and create

'til i make this world new

brown girl, brown girl

how are you so strong

'cause i got queens in my blood

to help push me along

*who protects
the brown and black babies*

because henrietta lacks didn't happen and tuskegee were just airmen

i am supposed to trust
white lab coats
white labs
white men
i am supposed to trust
because henrietta lacks didn't happen
tuskegee were just airmen
i am supposed to disclose
the fears of my soul
when i don't even know
where these voices are coming from
my family doesn't understand
it's all in my head
"just snap out of it
you wanna be depressed
just talk to the pastor
we didn't have these problems
when i was young"
they think i'm
deaf
crazy

dumb

ain't no black doctors

ain't no one who looks like me

who cares about me

the world is real specific

making sure i see

no brown people

with mds

i'm supposed to be

a strong black woman

and strength isn't depression

depression is weakness

i can't be weak

i've got too many depending on

my strength

so i carry the darkness

like a designer bag

heavy on my shoulder

heavy on my back

"bag lady you gon hurt your back

dragging all dem bags like that"

plus

i ain't crazy like that

i ain't homeless

jobless

i ain't rich either

therapy is for rich people

i dont want to pop a bunch

of pills

i've seen too many addicts

seen too many drug dependencies

i can take care of me

i can handle it

all on my own

'cuz it's just hard for me to trust

because henrietta lacks didn't happen

and

tuskegee were just airmen

e pluribus unum

i honor the souls
at the bottom of the sea
i honor the laborers shackled
and never set free
i honor the blood and the tears
that swung from trees
the raped and brutalized roots
that came before me
i honor the darkness
that swallowed some whole
that forged strength and resilience
no matter the toil

i honor the native tongues
ripped away and forbidden
the beliefs and spirit replaced with
white saints unbidden
i honor the indigenous
wiped from the earth
from blood-soaked soil
it labored and gave birth
to a mutated america
with greed and perversion
echoing in its mirth

i honor the migrant
with hands willing and able
that amidst immigration slurs
serve you from garden to table

i honor the underpaid
the overworked
the undervalued

i honor the union's
feet to cement
picket line strong
fight for a living wage
e pluribus unum

aunty maxine

black women have been
reclaiming time
since time began
since the first man
tried patriarchy
since the first slave ship
sailed with white supremacy
y'all call it strength
we call it magic
and though you appropriate
more than a kardashian clan
you can never have it

we reclaim our time
in dunham dances
with simone leaps
with nina melodies
and shelia beats
in the creases of
fabiola's paper
in janice's lens
in the souls of our daughters
the laughter of friends

in a kamala stare
a maxine glare
in the sheer regality of
shani-crowe-braided hair

we dig our feet firmly in this earth
gestating excellence
we give birth
to artistry and resistance
power and fame
reclaiming our
time
our titles
our names

have and the havenots

who protects
the brown and black babies
who's parents don't work for city hall
who aren't affluent or connected at all

who protects
the brown and black babies
when they start to look more like
young men and young ladies

who catches the ones that
fall through the cracks
created by lives full of
struggle and lack

who holds the cotillions
for the teens who are not in
jack and jill
who dream of making it to 25
and not being killed

who finds the links
for kids without mamas
in links
who is the collegiate plug

for children who want more
than to be called thugs

who stands in the gaps
to silence the claps
of guns with
poverty and hopelessness for caps

who loves the names
that gets resumés trashed
the bodies that are reduced to
commodified ass
the girls who are raped
and then are called fast
the minds unconcerned with credit
because they don't even have cash
who are undereducated and still pass
who's bellies know that food at home
doesn't last
who closes the gaps
so wide and so vast
the residue of racism
that infinitely lasts

age is more than just a number

we be tall
legs for days
curves and smiles
babies in bodies
that grew faster than
our minds can
we be alone
latch key
parents be working
or simply not there
we be mostly alone
looking for tribes
longing to be grown
because grown is safe
we be high school fresh
we be naive
we be fed on dreams of escape
of better
of abundance
we be vulnerable
we be victims
14 ain't on the same level
as 50
16 don't understand 40
19 is clueless to 30
we be prey
we ain't fast

we be children
we be unable to give consent
we need protection
we need soft places to fall
we need arms to hold us
we need hands to help us
cross the street
cross into adulthood
cross into the world
we need the cross not to shame us
we need more than urine on our laps
we need more than after-school pick up traps
we need our dreams to be more than bait
worm on hook
carrot dangled
fame and fortune offered
in exchange for statutory rape
we need you to show us
more than black woman hate

why you be so ready
to call us a lie
why you be so angry
when we tell the truth
did someone not
listen
believe
comfort
you

lineage lamentation

i don't remember the first time
my children
saw
me killed
but it wasn't last night
or last week
it's been a infinite loop of
having my blood splattered
on my children
like mothers before me
and after me
since booted white feet first
stepped on my shores
they've been killing me
for hundreds of years
in front of my babies
i've been
slaughtered
while protecting them
from the protectors
knife in hand
baby in womb
threats that were real
that made threats
echo in my mind
threaten my sanity
not every mother escapes
abuse

with her mind intact
protecting them i called out
for protection
and the knight riders dressed in blue
turned my home
into a cemetery
for my body
and the innocence
of my children
all of us dead
mamie till me
valerie castile me
open casket
anger kindling
speak my name
and those that came before me
the mothers
the slaughtered
the blood on peace officer's hands
long before korryn gains
long before charleena lyles
they've been killing me
while my babies watched
the same mouth that called for my death
will ask "why are black women so angry"
because you keep killing me

cultural bankruptcy

en el nombre
del padre
del hijo
y
del espíritu santo...
sometimes immigrants
wash culture
off their seeds
an uprooting
a transplanting
from fields of agave
to terra cotta pots
because gringolandia
requires sacrifices
the price of entry
is sometimes paid
in native tongues
ripped from your mouth
like weeds from the garden of
'merica
assimilation
for a green card
appropriation
the price for citizenship
a whitening

of flesh and sinew

spirit and soul

uncle sam fees for freedom surge

if you are black and brown

so sometimes

immigrants try to protect

by giving names that don't sound accented

by making english the only

instead of an addition

sometimes immigrants fight a lifetime

para el norte

only to find hate

as payment for hard work

bigotry

as payment for integrity

the death of culture in children

as payment for

protection

as payment for

"do better than me "

as payment for hope

and the children wander

lost

dancing between

a land that is memory

and a land that wants them

on the other side

of a wall

uncle steve

what does self hate look like

bald head mustache easter egg colored suit

what does an opportunist sound like

radio show host meeting with trump

what does bamboozlement read like

acting like a lady. thinking like a man.

following relationship advice from

a serial cheater.

what kind of jokes does a coon make

"enjoy your glass of brown water"

"enjoy your glass of lead poisoning"

"enjoy your glass of sick children"

"enjoy your glass of systemic racism"

"enjoy your glass of american

hate

neglect

classism"

"because me and mines drink champagne when we thristay"

"because i have made it standing on y'all black backs"

"because i have money and faux acceptance from the good

white folk"

"because i am not you. and you are not me"

"because when massa call i sholl nuff will step and fetch myself

to da white house. cuz massa just needs a chance.

hez a good massa.

hez gonna let me keep all my shows.

y'all hush alladat complaining.

i gotta get massa his covfefe"

thanks uncle steve. you're the best. we love you

dry ass judgement

where you gonna evacuate to

when you ain't got no car

ain't got no credit card

ain't got no cash

ain't got no expendable income

can't cover gouging prices

can't leave family

who can't move

because dialysis

because old age

because infants

or when the streets are flooded

when you are on the second floor

because the first is a pool of

water-filled with hopelessness and fear

poverty is often disguised as

hard working people

living check to check

without options

so while you watch flood waters

from the comfort of your dry ass

mayo-flavored home

some of us are watching g.o.t. on repeat

because the news

triggers

days of loved ones on rooftops

in sweltering august heat

days of death floating by

days of your history washed away

weeks of not knowing where your family was

months of your country ignoring your pain

and years of rebuilding laced with gentrification

everyone can't evacuate

harvey is not their fault

katrina was not our fault

failure of the levees was not our fault

the government acting

as it was created to

ignoring the suffering of black and brown

is not our fault

judging people who are fighting to survive

...that fault lives with you and your privilege

may our pain haunt your privileged peace

#prayersforhouston

with collective pain
and collective barriers
that some overcome
just to learn
there are more
hills to climb
more battles to fight

obliviate

so i've been in indy
celebrating my sister's 50th birthday
i have purposely not watched the news
so the rage would not consume me
i celebrated
loved
laughed
rode a mechanical bull
danced
lived in my happy bubble
i wonder if this what some
white americans feel like every day
purposefully oblivious to the world around them
to the hate around them
to systemic racism
to violence
to death
they just keep living
it must feel like this
minus the ache in my soul that is growing slowly
minus the visions of bodies flying over cars
minus the murder of an innocent woman
minus the knowledge that my country
condones slaughter
minus the hideous hate
how nice that must be
to not have to care
how peaceful
how white
#virginiasummer2017

a lesson in falling

i have fallen
countless times
feet in the air
skirt over my head
embarrassed
humiliated
i have looked into the faces
of people i thought loved me
to see them pleased at where
i landed
where rock bottom had found me
saw them looking down at me
in a hole
afraid
and they never reached
to pull me up
pull me out
or even shout
to not give up
i had to cheer myself on
i am clumsy
i fall often
it's disorientating
falling
not knowing
which way is up
can you catch yourself
how badly will this fall hurt
how long will it take you to recover
asking all of this in the seconds

between the trip
the mistake
the bump
and the landing
lately i've noticed
that i'm not falling down as much
i'm falling up
falling forward
falling into place
the landings are softer
when i don't fight it
when i know it's inevitable
i have taught myself how to fall
so i don't hurt so badly

but i learn more quickly
teach yourself how to fall
teach your babies how to fall
i promise you
it won't take your breath away
it will help you breathe

i took my ancestors with me

i entered the plantation

like i do with most moments in my life

divided. dual.

living paradox

one foot black

one foot latina

i entered the plantation

both owner and owned

both master and slave

both free and forever captive

both entitled and lost

alone and holding my daughter's hand

angry and in awe

i entered the plantation

with gratitude and rage

wanting to pray and scream

to cherish and burn it to the ground

it was all too much

the earth they walked on

the air they breathed

the spanish moss

hanging from branches

did my ancestors hang from them too

the bricks in the walls of the big house

made by slaves

i touched them slowly

reverently

imagining the hands that

made them

laid them

the hands that were the foundation
of that house
of my family
of my country
this place
where my ancestors walked
where slaves rebelled
where slaves were executed
this place
designed by a free man of color
furniture carved by a free man of color
owned by a free man
who enslaved people of color
this place
of indigo and sugar cane
of senegal and france
louisiana purchase
humans purchased
the earth i stood on
purchased
with the blood
that flows through my veins
i left the plantation
with my daughter's hand in mine
head high
heart heavy
wanting reparations
wanting birthrights
wanting sobs begging for my
forgiveness
for my children's

forgiveness
i wanted to scream
get off my land
it's mine a thousand times over
payment has been made
a thousand lives over
i walked in with questions
i walked out with answers
this place
both beginning and end
life and death
i found completion in the air
i inhaled
survival
strength
resistance
resilience
beneath my feet
i found
hope
healing
new found hatred
my existence
my children's existence
my people's existence
is an eternal jihad
i left with a new fire
with the heat of a thousand suns
with the cries of a thousands souls
i left
and i took my ancestors with me

dear body,

yesterday sandria washington posted a video about a woman coming to terms with feeling too tall most of her life. i reflected on feeling too tall, not wanting to wear heels, feeling like i just took up too much space. i realized that for probably more than half of my 40 years i have not loved you, my body.

early on you were too much. you were too tall, too much boob, too much leg, just too much for a teen to deal with. i didn't know how to walk in the glory that was you. you made me afraid when you called attention to me that i didn't want and that i couldn't process. you made me look like a woman when i was still very much a girl. part of me hates you for that.

in early adulthood i didn't pay enough attention to you. i didn't revel in youth, freedom, or in beauty that i had no idea i possessed. i was busy learning how to be an adult. learning how to find my passion. i took you for granted. i didn't celebrate you.

then, in the wrong marriage, that came with the wrong kind of love, i did my best to diminish you, to not draw too much attention to you. he would become annoyed and angry when too many men noticed me. so i tried not to shine too brightly because the better i felt about you and i, the worse he felt about himself and then the worse my world became.

then mini humans came. and with each pregnancy i marveled in your strength. in all of this magic that you had. feeling like a goddess. making a life. birth and breast-feeding with just the beginning. being a mother transformed how i looked at you. you no longer belonged to just me. how i thought about you no longer belonged to just me. how i talked about you no longer belonged to just me. in fact i began to no longer really understand what me was. i was lost between mother and woman. searching for ways to join them.

i had always felt like i had taken up too much space. too big, too loud, too bright. and now here you and i were, me and my body, bigger and bolder. somehow i started to focus just on what i thought were your imperfections. it wasn't even that i struggled to find my own beauty, i just stopped looking for it. i stopped looking at you. as depression often does, the cycle spun around and around, feeding upon itself. the darker the darkness became.

without knowing how we got there, there we were. you and i. in a rut. depressed. feeling more than alone.

not feeling strong or powerful or beautiful. feeling functional at best.
then an amazing thing happened.

my bestie put down his paint brushes and picked up a camera. he took some pictures of me and i saw myself differently. i saw some woman who looked pretty dope. i saw rolls that i hated looking like soft love. i saw arms that made homes for mini humans. i saw feet that could dance away pain. i saw a belly that has never been flat but always been a magnet for 3 year olds to bury their faces in, full of tears or crashing in for a hug.

and i saw sexy.

for the first time in a long time i saw sexy.

i saw the small of my back arching. i saw a butt that babies helped me grow. i saw breasts that after 3 nursing children finally were mine again.

i saw hips that could sway to any beat. and thick thighs that could save lives.

7 years ago, i trusted someone to show me, you. and you and i have never been the same. i'm sorry for not seeing you sooner. for not running naked in water fountains in college. or for being afraid of wearing 5 inch heels. i'm sorry for not pampering you, thinking that only single digit sizes deserved attention. i'm sorry for speaking about you with less than loving words. for not letting you dance more often. for turning the lights off when we made love.

i'm sorry for hating you.

thank you for always loving me.

i don't have to promise to love you. because i already do.

immensely.

i do promise to say nice things to you more often.

i promise to stand in the mirror and look at you.

fresh out the shower and tell you that your jiggle is

marvelous.

i promise to wear spanx less often

to let you breathe

to not try to conform you into a body type you aren't

i promise to wear a bikini every summer

they are not just for a size 4

your belly deserves to be summer brown too.

i promise to eat more veggies and drink

more water.

to find ways to move daily.

even if it's just doing a cumbia down the aisles at target.

i promise to get more massages

use great products

take more nude photos

and to leave the lights on when we get busy

i promise to not spend the next 50 or more years hating
you, reminiscing on youth long gone
but to be grateful for every day i have you, my body.

Thank you to all of the Backers
who made this possible...

Adrienne
Aisha Samuel
AJ Deloney
Alicia Hudson
Amena Johnson
Andrea Carvalhais Shelby
Angela Foudray
Angelica Callanta
Antoinette Laws
Autumn Dawkins
b.terry
Betty West
Bill Boyd
Brandi Friedman
Brian Alexander
Brice Kessler
Carla Carrillo
Catriese Henning
Charmaine N. Ward
Cheryl Hall-Russell
Christie Gooden Magee
Danjuma Gaskin
Darren Lipman
David Grant
DDE
Derek Phipps
Dr. Michael D. Bradley
Dr. Michele Levy
Ebony Ambrose
Erskine Cunningham
Felicia Davis
Fredrick Berry
Gemma Wilson
Gerald E. Jones

Geri Redd
Gina Colello
Gregory O. Ajose
Gwen Carter
Heather Hendee
Hector Lastra
Henry alvarez
Isabell Ciszewski
J. Stuckey
Jacklyn Egipciaco
Jada
James Derek Oliphant
James Dirden
Jenna R. Hatton-Cobb
Jennifer Cardona
Jerel Jackson
Jesse Marsh
Jessica Mancilla
Jihad F Saleh
jminding@yahoo.com
Juval Scott
Kacey Martin-Johnson
Kamilah Turner
Katrinka Markowitz
Kellee Knighten Hough
Kemba Hendrix
Kimberly Hall
Kimberly Hooks Blanks
La-Shawn Hill
Lee Bey
Lisa Austin
Lisa Leaheey
Loey Kelvington Allingham
Lori Watts-Branch

M Marshall
Malik M.L. Williams
Marcellus H Moore Jr.
Marqueal Jordan
Marvin Jarrett
Maureen Duffy
Maya Wyche
Melissa Wojcik
meredith wood
Meshanda L. McKenzie
Michelle Davis-Dash, MD
Michelle Hood
Miriam K. Melvin
Naamayth Goins
Niesy Dunn
Niki Gee
Patricia Raspberry
Paul Q. Fortson
Randi Craigen
Randy Conner
Regis Inge
Renee
Renee Lockett
Rhiannon Gaiter
Richard Holloway
Ricki Proper
Robert Lane
S. C. Compton
Sanders C. Sonya
Santino Romero
Sara S. Marsh
Sarah Frandson Dorfman
Sarah Jolie
Sarah Schar

Sheila Robinson
Sheri Smith Clayborn
Sideeka Ryan
Siete Saudades
Stephanie Graham
Stephanie Perez
TaiScott Ponder
Tamiko Umoren
Tarence Jones
Teela Williams
Tennille McGee Parris
The Harris Family
The Stubbs Family
Trimiko Melancon
Trina Blunt
Troy K. Venning (Pastor Troy)
Venus Boutte
Will Dailey
William Murray
Yaritza G Burton
Zenzile Powell

Leslé Honoré is a "Blaxican" Poet. Mother of three phenomenal mini-humans; Sage, Solomon and Scarlett. A freedom fighter and Spirit Writer. Born and raised in Gardena California by her father Louis Honoré Sr., a native of New Orleans and her mother Rosalba Honoré, who was born in Sinaloa Culiacan Mexico, and immigrated to the US when she was 15. Leslé began writing in grammar school and has never stopped. She attended Xavier University in New Orleans studying English Literature where she was editor of Xavier's literary journal, New Voices. Leslé has lived in Chicago for almost 18 years, considers herself a Chicagoan based on her love of House Music, being able to drive Lower Wacker and not get lost, and knowing that Harold's Chicken is better than Uncle Remus. She has worked in the non-profit field for almost twenty years, advocating for under-served youth.

Poetry has always been how Leslé has expressed herself. Focusing mainly on social injustice, she hopes that through her work she can help give voices to people who are often silenced, unheard and feel invisible.

Leslé believes that HBCUs, Tacos and Gumbo without kale can save the world.

LesleHonore.com

UPCOMING PROJECTS by
Lesle' Honore'

Letters and Lagniappe

and

Tears and Triumph

PRODUCTIONS

CPSIA information can be obtained
at www.ICGtesting.com
Printed in the USA
BVHW040353240321
603162BV00013B/51